Can You Hear The Music?

David Campton

A SAMUEL FRENCH ACTING EDITION

SAMUEL FRENCH

FOUNDED 1830

SAMUELFRENCH-LONDON.CO.UK
SAMUELFRENCH.COM

CHARACTERS

Pricklemouse, sharp and inclined to take any remark personally

Fussmouse, bossy but nervous

Housemouse, down to earth

Eldermouse, staid and pompous

Gigglemouse, talkative but not very bright

Tattymouse, completely deaf, but tries to cover up the fact

The action takes place in an enormous loft

PRODUCTION NOTES

Production can be as simple or as elaborate as imagination and resources allow, bearing in mind that any scenery and properties should be about ten times normal size, and that a mouse tail is as long as the mouse itself.

In the original production the tails were made from foam plastic pipe lagging and mouse ears were sewn on to balaclavas. Seats were a cotton reel and a matchbox, while a line of washing was stretched between a six-foot high pencil and an equally large brown paper parcel.

The music can be recorded, but a live musician (playing a simple instrument such as a recorder) can respond more flexibly to what is happening on stage. In the original production one basic tune was repeated as a waltz, a tango, a march and a lullaby.

D.C.

CAN YOU HEAR THE MUSIC?

A loft seen from the point of view of a mouse

There is a pile of lumber over and around which mice can scramble and hide. At first, six Mice are sitting very still and listening

Eldermouse There!

Fussmouse Hah!

Pricklemouse Shush! We're listening for . . .

Fussmouse Nothing.

Pricklemouse Nothing?

Fussmouse At all.

Gigglemouse Ah!

Housemouse Not—music?

Fussmouse Certainly not music.

Housemouse It sounded like music to me.

Fussmouse Wind through a mousehole. This place is full of draughts.

Eldermouse Certainly something blowing through something. It reminded me of . . .

Fussmouse Nothing.

Eldermouse How could anything remind me of nothing?

Fussmouse If it was nothing, it couldn't remind you of anything.

Gigglemouse (*giggling*) Almost anything can remind me of something.

Pricklemouse Almost anything reminds you of just one thing.

Housemouse To me it suggested distant waves breaking on a tropical shore.

Fussmouse When did you hear waves on a tropical shore?

Housemouse I can dream, can't I?

Fussmouse To me it meant water.

Pricklemouse Water? Really?

Fussmouse Dark, deep, fast-flowing water—that has drowning in it.

Pricklemouse You never did have much of an ear for music, did you?

Fussmouse (*shouting*) There was no music!

Tattymouse (*suddenly aware of something going on*) Oh, were you speaking to me? I agree, of course.

Pricklemouse I know what I heard.

Fussmouse You heard nothing. Nothing! Nothing!!

A distant phrase of music is played on a simple wind instrument such as a bamboo pipe or recorder

There is an awkward pause

Tattymouse (*aware of the strained atmosphere if not of its cause*) Have I said the wrong thing again?

Fussmouse I didn't hear that, either.

Tattymouse I should have said "really". Really is the answer to everything—especially when one hasn't heard the question.

Gigglemouse Could it have been the lost chord?

Fussmouse I'll tell you what it is. It's cheese in the trap.

Pricklemouse Very poetic.

Housemouse I don't understand. Who's talking about cheese?

Fussmouse I said "trap". Understand "trap"? Nibble, nibble—bang!

Eldermouse Please! One doesn't mention such things. Remember Tattymouse's dear departed.

Tattymouse (*understanding that she is being talked about*) Ah, yes. Just what I was going to say.

Pricklemouse Fussmouse has been babbling again.

Eldermouse I think Fussmouse is frightened.

Pricklemouse Fussmouse is always frightened.

Tattymouse Is this a game? Better count me out. I've been no good at games since ... well ...

Fussmouse Don't any of you remember what Grandmouse told us?

Housemouse Grandmouse?

Fussmouse About The Piper?

Eldermouse Oh, The Piper. Really, Fussy. Have you been making all this to-do because of what Grandmouse once said about The Piper?

Gigglemouse Everybody knows that was just another old Grandmouse story.

Fussmouse Everybody?

Gigglemouse Even I know that. She said The Piper comes for those who haven't behaved themselves. Though I don't suppose the old thing had anything to do with a Piper in her life.

Fussmouse She'd never have lived to tell us if she had. Those who see The Piper never do.

Pricklemouse Tall tales and tarrididdles. She heard them at her Grandmouse's knee—who got them from *her* Grandmouse. Who believes a Grandmouse these days?

Fussmouse The shivers up and down my spine tell me it was true.

Housemouse Do you believe in the Sandmouse and the Flower Fairies, too? Anyway, The Piper piped away rats, not mice.

Fussmouse The principle is the same. Toot, toot, toot and away they went.

Eldermouse We're still here.

Fussmouse For how long?

Eldermouse For as long as we choose. Down there they'd like to be rid of us, but they won't be. Ever. We're wise to their cats and their traps and their poisoned bait. They'll have to bring in something very different to be rid of us.

Fussmouse Perhaps they have.

Gigglemouse You're just saying that to frighten me.

Fussmouse I hope I have. Because if you're frightened, you may take precautions.

Gigglemouse Everybody tries to frighten me. Don't nibble between meals, they say. Sugar is bad for the heart and teeth. And if you grow too fat to run, the cat could get you. Now it's "Music can damage your health". Well, I won't be frightened of anything else. So there!

Fussmouse It's for your own good.

Gigglemouse That's what you always say when you're suggesting something horrid.

Fussmouse Do you *want* The Piper to get you?

Gigglemouse Oh!

Fussmouse Do you want to die?

Gigglemouse Don't!

Fussmouse Or worse?

Gigglemouse I feel sick.

Pricklemouse That's not fright: it's lump sugar.

Gigglemouse Whatever it is, it's turning my inside over.

Eldermouse Don't be a silly, Giggle. There's no such thing as a Piper. There never was.

A phrase of pipe music, nearer, followed by a breathless pause

Housemouse What was That?
Gigglemouse Coming this way!

There is a sudden panic among the Mice, who scamper about in all directions—with the exception of Tattymouse, who is merely bewildered

Fussmouse Scatter.
Pricklemouse Scramble.
Eldermouse Heads down.
Housemouse Hide.
Gigglemouse Where?
Pricklemouse How?
Gigglemouse From what?
Eldermouse From That.
Fussmouse It.
Housemouse Here.
Gigglemouse Help!

With the exception of Tattymouse all are now out of sight behind pieces of lumber

Tattymouse Am I missing something?
Pricklemouse What now?
Gigglemouse What can we do?
Tattymouse Is this another game?
Eldermouse Don't lose your heads. Once heads are lost, the rest is bound to follow.
Tattymouse It can't have been the cat. Whenever the cat is near my whiskers bristle and my hair stands on end. But nothing is bristling and nothing is standing on end.

The Mice peep out from behind lumber

Housemouse Can you hear anything now?
Pricklemouse Only Tattymouse, talking to herself.
Housemouse We did hear, didn't we? It was music, wasn't it?
Pricklemouse Could it have been the telephone wires singing?
Eldermouse Could it have been the gurgle of a waste pipe?
Tattymouse Look on the bright side. That's what I always say.
Fussmouse (*grudgingly*) It was music all right.

Tattymouse My late lamented used to say that, too. Before he became late.

Gigglemouse Oooh!

Tattymouse And lamented.

Eldermouse But was it *the* music?

Tattymouse Look on the bright side. Just a thought.

Eldermouse We've all heard music in our time — even Tatty, when she could hear anything at all. But was that Him?

Gigglemouse Him! Oh!

Eldermouse The music came and went. We're all still here and none the worse.

Fussmouse Forewarned is forearmed, I say.

Eldermouse If that wasn't His music, who cares whose music it was? So why are we cowering here like timorous beasties?

Fussmouse I believe in being on the safe side.

Eldermouse I believe in facing facts.

Pricklemouse What facts?

Fussmouse We've all been told what to expect from The Piper.

Eldermouse If there *is* a Piper.

Fussmouse You know there's a Piper.

Eldermouse We only have Grandmouse's word.

Housemouse After all, hearing's believing.

Eldermouse Heard what? A piece on a penny whistle? (*Ironically*) Ha. Ha.

Pricklemouse No more than a simple tune, after all.

Housemouse What harm did a tune on a penny whistle do to anybody? (*Nervously*) Ha-ha.

Gigglemouse It does seem silly — being afraid of a tune. Especially such a toot-toot sort of tune.

Fussmouse I — could have been — a little — hasty.

Pricklemouse (*heavily*) Ha. Ha.

Gigglemouse Do you mean ha ha or ha-ha?

Pricklemouse I mean ha-ha-ha.

Gigglemouse Ha-ha-ha?

Housemouse Ha-ha-ha.

Laughter becomes infectious and grows. Laughing, the Mice emerge from their hiding-places

Tattymouse Back already? Have a jolly game?

Eldermouse As the man said — "Blow your pipe until you burst".

Fussmouse That's an old joke. And it was silly when the man first made it.

Pricklemouse Almost as silly as being afraid of a—of—a . . .

Pricklemouse is stopped by pipe music. For a second or so quiet is restored. Then the laughter is resumed as Eldermouse baits the unseen Piper and Gigglemouse giggles encouragement

Eldermouse Hey, Piper, where did you learn to play?

Pricklemouse Or is it something you just picked up?

Eldermouse If I were you, I'd put it back where I found it.

Pricklemouse How do you make a living with piping like that?

Eldermouse Are you paid to play or to go away?

Tattymouse They say laughing is good for the lungs.

Pricklemouse Pardon me, your instrument needs tuning.

Tattymouse Yes. That's what they say.

Gigglemouse If that's music, I can take it or leave it.

Eldermouse I'd rather leave it.

Pricklemouse What do you say, Fussmouse?

Fussmouse Me?

Pricklemouse Still afraid?

Fussmouse (*bolder*) What—me? Afraid? Hey, Piper. Piper. What was that tune again?

Pipe music repeats the phrase

Pricklemouse That sounds like flatulence to me.

Housemouse (*a long low sigh*) Aaaaaah . . .

Pricklemouse Eh?

The laughter dies

Fussmouse What was that? What did she say?

Housemouse The soft south whispers promise through the indigo night.

Eldermouse What?

Housemouse In the rigging above us are stars shining bright, like clusters of diamonds caught up in a net, while lovers' sighs mingle in murmured duet.

Fussmouse Housemouse?

Gigglemouse What does that mean?

Housemouse seems to have fallen into a trance, oblivious to anything except the music

Housemouse More. More. All my life I have waited for that call—vibrating through my being like a maestro playing on my heartstrings. Again. Again. Play it again.

Pricklemouse Who on earth is she talking to?

Fussmouse I don't know, and I don't think I want to know.

Eldermouse You—Housemouse—can hear me?

Housemouse What matter mere words when the message is clear? I am waiting, my love. Oh, my love I am here.

Pricklemouse That doesn't make sense.

Gigglemouse I thought I was the one who doesn't talk sense.

Housemouse That plaintive melody, drawing one to the far yonder where birds of paradise play against eternal blue and I am yours and you are mine 'til all the seas run dry.

Fussmouse That's what the music can do.

Tattymouse Fancy.

Fussmouse I warned you, didn't I? "Don't listen," I said. Didn't I say that?

Tattymouse (*nodding agreement*) Ah.

Fussmouse This is like talking to a brick wall.

Tattymouse Perhaps another time.

Housemouse A loud call. A clear call. That cannot be denied: (*She begins to drift away like a sleepwalker*)

Fussmouse (*trying to hold her back*) Not that way. It's not safe out there: not what you imagine waiting for you.

Housemouse Neither fetters nor bars can hold us apart, my love.

Eldermouse She seems to have made up her mind.

Fussmouse Or lost it. Give me a hand, somebody. Listen to me, House, not to that siren song. Once you go to it, you'll never come back.

Housemouse I have immortal longings in me.

Fussmouse There's nothing immortal about you. You'll die.

Eldermouse But happy. Perhaps that's the best way to go after all.

Fussmouse She won't be happy dead. She won't be anything except dead.

Housemouse (*receding*) If music be the food of love, save me the waltz . . .

Fussmouse They're not even your own words.

Pricklemouse Can you think of any better?

Housemouse is now out of sight

Fussmouse Come back.

Housemouse (*off; distantly*) With the wind and the rain on my fur. . .

There is a slight pause while the remaining Mice look at each other

Gigglemouse Has she gone?

Tattymouse (*trying a non-committal expression to sum up an incomprehensible situation*) That's the way it goes.

Pricklemouse How is it that Tattymouse, with no idea of what is going on, manages to say exactly the wrong thing? Not *it*, Tatty. Housemouse. And, as for going, we may not know where she's gone, but we have a good idea of what will happen when she gets there.

Tattymouse (*nodding and smiling*) That's what I always say.

Pricklemouse Oh, give me strength!

Gigglemouse Was it really the music?

Pricklemouse Do you suppose it might have been something she ate?

Gigglemouse I once ate a Valentine card, but that was an accident. I didn't even know it was a Valentine card until afterwards. I felt peculiar for hours, but it didn't have me behaving like Housemouse.

Fussmouse Well — now we know.

Eldermouse Do we?

Fussmouse At least we've been alerted. We know what that Piper can do.

Eldermouse It seemed to me that Housemouse wasn't hearing what we were hearing. To her it was a different tune.

Fussmouse In future we mustn't listen to *any* music.

Gigglemouse If it comes, can we help listening?

Fussmouse We've minds of our own, haven't we?

Gigglemouse Didn't House have a mind of her own? She knew an awful lot about domestic economy.

Pricklemouse A head so full of romantic twaddle was bound to get turned sooner or later.

Gigglemouse I wasn't aware her head *was* full of romantic twaddle.

Pricklemouse Well, you're aware now.

Gigglemouse She never said anything romantic to me.

Pricklemouse She wouldn't, would she?

Gigglemouse When we did talk confidentially — which wasn't very often; because between you and me she didn't consider my brain among the brightest: not that I blame her because I'd have thought that too if I'd thought about it at all—well, it was all stuff like babies and food and what all the best places looked like with wall-to-wall this and floor-to-ceiling the other. Nothing remotely romantic, unless you find do-it-yourself plumbing romantic. Nothing to do with Eastern promise or moonlight or losing the world for love. She certainly never mentioned music, soft or otherwise.

Fussmouse I'd be obliged if you wouldn't either.

Gigglemouse Funny that it should have reminded her of tropical nights.

Eldermouse Funny is as funny does.

Gigglemouse To me it sounded more like the tinkle of ice.

Eldermouse Ice?

Gigglemouse You know—in glasses.

Pricklemouse The which in what?

Gigglemouse I often dream of ice in glasses—with expensive drinks, too, of course, and things like cherries and olives on sticks in them. That's what the music meant to me.

Fussmouse Gigglemouse!

Gigglemouse Sorry. That's the way my mixed-up mind puts things together, but we can't help what we dream, can we? Mmmm. Yes. With a touch of tango in the background. Doesn't a tango always make you want to swoon? Di-dum. Di-dum. Di-dum-dum-dum. Ooooh! Swooning seems to make the steps easier to follow. Didn't you hear a tango?

Fussmouse No more than you did. That's the way The Piper works. He lets you hear what you want to hear.

A strain of pipe music is heard

Gigglemouse There it is again. Di-dum. Dum-dum.

Fussmouse Don't let her go on. We don't want another accident, do we? I said—do we?

Tattymouse You're so right.

Gigglemouse Di-dum-dum-dum. Someone must be giving a party.

Fussmouse How can we keep her from joining it?

Gigglemouse Hark! Wasn't that a champagne cork popping?

Eldermouse It was not. It was . . . (*He is unable to say the word*) It was . . .

Gigglemouse But it couldn't have been anything else. Nothing pops quite like a champagne cork. Except another champagne cork. I love that pop, pop, pop, pop, pop.

Tattymouse I see what you mean.

Gigglemouse And after all that popping, it's a pity to waste the wine.

Tattymouse Decidedly.

Fussmouse Distract her attention. Bring her back to the here and now.

Music

Gigglemouse (*listening*) Mmm?

Fussmouse Walk her up and down. That ought to bring her to her senses.

Pricklemouse What senses?

Eldermouse Come on then.

With one on either side of Gigglemouse, Fussmouse and Eldermouse walk her up and down as though trying to sober her

Gigglemouse (*listening*) What are you trying to say?

Eldermouse Don't worry. We're taking care of you. Walk.

Fussmouse You're in safe hands, Gigglemouse.

Eldermouse With us.

Fussmouse With friends.

Gigglemouse Some of my best friends have continental-sounding names—like Fabergé and Cartier and Tiffany. With addresses.in Bond Street and Fifth Avenue and—what is that rue in Paris?

Fussmouse Slow down. I can't keep up.

Pricklemouse She's in another world.

Fussmouse Bring her back to this one. Look at us, Giggle.

Eldermouse Please.

Gigglemouse (*responding to Eldermouse's touch*) Please! (*She giggles*) Some partners are so quick to take advantage.

Eldermouse Would slapping her face do any good?

Fussmouse Only if it rendered her completely unconscious.

Pricklemouse And the difference would never show.

Gigglemouse I always say what is a tiara without a title?

Pricklemouse Is that a riddle?

Gigglemouse The two go together like kind hearts and coronets. If I have a little weakness, it's for a marquis or an earl. I'd just die for a title.

Fussmouse You very well may.

Tattymouse I do like to see you all enjoying yourselves.

Music

Gigglemouse Hark!

Fussmouse Think!

Pricklemouse No use. The bright lights are gleaming in her beady little eyes.

Gigglemouse The major domo is announcing the company. "Sir and Lady ..." "Lord and Lady ..." Music to the ears.

Pricklemouse There's no way she'll be turned aside.

Gigglemouse Stand aside you peasants. Wasn't that worth waiting to hear?

Gigglemouse sails out to dazzle an imagined company

Fussmouse It's only The Piper calling.

Gigglemouse (*off; distantly*) "Your Highness ..."

Fussmouse She doesn't know what she's doing.

Eldermouse Don't panic. I'll go after her.

Pricklemouse (*incredulously*) You never will!

Eldermouse Sound the advance and stand by to cheer. The cavalry is coming.

Pricklemouse You couldn't be such a fool.

Eldermouse To the rescue.

Pricklemouse You're no knight in armour.

Eldermouse Into the valley of death rode the six hundred.

Fussmouse Oh, no, no, no.

Pricklemouse In the first place there's only one of you. And in the second place you'd all go the same way—you and the other five hundred and ninety-nine. There are no return tickets issued for that ride.

Eldermouse I'll bring her back if it's the last thing I do.

Pricklemouse It will be.

Eldermouse How can mouse die better than facing fearful odds? Stand aside, worms, there's no time to lose.

Fussmouse You think you can hear the clink of medals, but it's that same old Piper's tune.

Eldermouse It is a far, far better thing that I do ...

Eldermouse marches out, starry-eyed, to the music

Fussmouse Honestly, Giggle isn't worth the sacrifice.

Pricklemouse That's no sacrifice. It's the ultimate in self-indulgence.

Eldermouse (*off; distantly*) Let me like a soldier fall.

Pricklemouse (*shouting*) Stage-struck lunatic!

Fussmouse Another.

Tattymouse Why is everybody leaving?

Fussmouse Half of us gone.

Tattymouse Is it something I said?

Pricklemouse You?

Tattymouse I know I'm always saying the wrong thing.

Pricklemouse As if that mattered now.

Tattymouse Oh, why do I do it?

Pricklemouse Why did any of them do it?

Fussmouse They couldn't help themselves.

Pricklemouse Nonsense.

Tattymouse Eh?

Pricklemouse (*shouting*) Nonsense! I said nonsense.

Tattymouse I know, I know. There's something ludicrous about pretending to understand when you don't. But eccentricity attracts more sympathy than disability. Better seem dotty than deaf.

Pricklemouse What are you on about?

Fussmouse There's always something one is prepared to die for.

Pricklemouse Either of you.

Fussmouse The Piper caught them all on their weakest point.

Pricklemouse The bigger fools them.

Fussmouse We may not know what our weak points are. But we're likely to find out. With a practical demonstration.

Tattymouse I wish ...

Fussmouse I wouldn't if I were you.

Tattymouse That the clock could be turned back. That my ears were more than decoration.

Fussmouse Know when you're well off. You're safer as you are.

Tattymouse Ah, well ...

Fussmouse We're all safe as long as we ignore the music.

Pricklemouse What happens when it starts again?

Fussmouse Fill your ears with something else. Anything. Drown it before it drowns us.

Pricklemouse How?

Fussmouse Sing.

Pricklemouse Us?
Fussmouse And dance.
Pricklemouse I can't.
Fussmouse You will.
Pricklemouse I've never done either.
Fussmouse You'll learn.

Pipe music is heard

Quick. Start a song. Any song. "The Old Cat".

Fussmouse starts to sing. Pricklemouse joins in. Tattymouse watches, wondering

Pricklemouse (*together* "Have you heard? The old cat's dead.
Fussmouse *singing*) Fell from a tree and landed on his
head.
The sparrow he was stalking flew
away and said
"The garden will be safer now the old
cat's dead."

Fussmouse Dance!
Pricklemouse At the same time?
Fussmouse (*together*) "Can you imagine a cat so dim?
Pricklemouse Tried to catch his dinner by the
water's brim.
Jumped into the pond but forgot he
couldn't swim.
Once he ate the fishes now the fish
eat him."

Tattymouse It's very decent of you to try to cheer me up.
Pricklemouse Is The Piper still playing?
Fussmouse Don't stop to find out.
Fussmouse (*together*) "The old cat's knocking at heaven's
Pricklemouse gate.
All because of something on the old
cat's plate.
The old cat's dinner was our
poisoned bait.
Now the old cat's dicky with the bait
he ate."

Pricklemouse (*panting*) I'm breathless.

Tattymouse applauds

Tattymouse Very entertaining. I feel much better now.
Pricklemouse Thank you, thank you.
Fussmouse (*singing*)   "This is the tale of the old dead cat.
                              Cats don't come any deader than that.

Fussmouse notices that Pricklemouse is no longer singing and dancing but is still bowing to an imaginary audience. Fussmouse's singing slows to a stop

                    So—please put—a penny in—the old man's
                    hat
                    To pay for the coffin of . . ."
Pricklemouse (*blowing kisses*) So kind. So kind.
Fussmouse You stopped. The music . . .
Pricklemouse To your true artiste there's no music to match the sound of hands meeting hands.
Fussmouse That's only Tattymouse, and she didn't hear a note.
Pricklemouse (*bowing*) Such a beautiful audience.
Fussmouse Quick. Another verse . . . (*singing*) "The old cat's lost all nine of its lives . . ." Join in, then.
Pricklemouse Don't you try to steal my thunder. You supporting casts are all the same. Jealous, every one.
Fussmouse Jealous of what?
Pricklemouse Afraid to let me shine, because your eyes can't bear the dazzle.
Fussmouse Pull yourself together, Prickle.
Pricklemouse Out there they know better. I give my all, and they respond with rapture. Listen to that applause. My public. They love me. Hark.

Music

Fussmouse Stop this.
Pricklemouse The crowd is calling.
Fussmouse There's nobody calling for you but the undertaker.
Pricklemouse "Encore", they cry. For the star of the show.
Fussmouse You'll be star turn at your own funeral—and there'll be no encores after that.
Pricklemouse I come truly to life only to the sound of an ovation. Hear it now. Like the crash of surf on an infinite shore.

Pricklemouse starts to drift away but is held back by Fussmouse

Fussmouse (*trying to hold back Pricklemouse*) Delusions.

Pricklemouse (*struggling to break free*) Are you trying to muscle in on my triumph?

Fussmouse Tattymouse, help me to hold this idiot back before it's too late.

Pricklemouse Typical envy.

Fussmouse I can't hold on.

Tattymouse Is it a new dance?

Fussmouse Join in.

Tattymouse I can't hear any music.

Fussmouse Lucky you.

Pricklemouse They're throwing bouquets out there. I won't be denied my moments of glory. I want my flowers.

Fussmouse (*still wrestling*) If you're not careful, you'll get them — by the hearseful. Tatty . . .

Tattymouse I can't follow those steps.

Pricklemouse Those flowers are mine by divine right. With curtain after curtain. But they won't hold the curtain for ever.

Fussmouse I'm tiring. Take over from me.

Pricklemouse Who are you to keep me from my darlings?

Fussmouse Please!

Tattymouse (*applauding*) You're both very good.

Pricklemouse Hear them clamour for more. More! And they shall have it.

Tattymouse You should do it more often.

Pricklemouse Unhand me. (*She kicks Fussmouse*)

Fussmouse (*letting go*) Ouch! I'm warning you. One step outside and you're as good as cat's meat.

Pricklemouse Always quit on the crest of the wave. (*To an imaginary audience*) I am yours, darlings. Yours all the way . . .

Pricklemouse makes a sweeping exit to music

Fussmouse Why should you crave the cheers of a crowd? Solid, reliable straight-up-and-down you. What fires have you been banking down all these years?

Pricklemouse (*off; distantly*) Autographs?

Tattymouse A very clever exit, if I may say so. I wondered how that act was going to end. It *was* all part of the piece, wasn't it? Nothing to do with me this time? After all, I didn't say a thing except to encourage you.

Fussmouse Perhaps I worry too much about others.

Tattymouse This loft looks bigger with only the two of us in it.

Fussmouse Looking after others becomes a habit after a while.

Tattymouse Will they be coming back soon?

Fussmouse Perhaps I've always been too ready to shoulder their burdens.

Tattymouse We'll miss them if they don't.

Fussmouse I've never really considered what *I* want.

Tattymouse I still miss my Charleymouse, you know. Even after all this time.

Fussmouse Perhaps it's time I did consider myself for a change.

Tattymouse He was a fool and his belly was bigger than his brain, but there are plenty like that.

Fussmouse So what do I really want? After a lifetime of putting others first, what am I missing most? What?

Tattymouse Though, if there are plenty like him, why couldn't I find another to take his place?

Fussmouse H'm. At least if there's nothing the music can promise me, I should be safe from its blandishments. Shouldn't I?

Tattymouse Wherever I am, there's always an empty space where he ought to be.

Fussmouse You can't tempt me, Piper. So stuff that in your pipe and smoke it. I'm safe from you.

Tattymouse But I shouldn't be rattling on so.

Fussmouse Safety! Is that the weak link? Is that what He might offer?

Tattymouse I don't want to trouble anyone with my troubles.

Fussmouse Who'd stick their neck into a noose just to feel safe? I'm not that sort of idiot. I hope. Not me. Oh, no, no, no, no, no. Unthinkable. So why think it? Think about something else instead. Anything. Tattymouse, talk to me.

Tattymouse Eh?

Fussmouse (*shouting*) Talk!

Tattymouse Did you say talk?

Fussmouse I said talk.

Tattymouse I have been talking.

Fussmouse Carry on talking.

Tattymouse Were you listening?

Fussmouse No, but don't let that stop you now.

Tattymouse I never expect anyone to listen to me. I'm always harking back to you-know-who. Such a bore. He had some good points, but it's the little irritations I miss most. There were plenty of those to miss. I won't list them. I'd only bore you more. Anyway they all ceased to matter after he trod on the trap.

Fussmouse Trap!

Tattymouse If I warned him once, I warned him a thousand times.

Fussmouse Did you have to mention traps?

Tattymouse I kept telling him there's no such thing as a safe trap.

Fussmouse Trap!

Tattymouse But he was so sure he knew all there was to know about traps.

Fussmouse Traps!

Tattymouse Obstinate. I told him. "If it was safe, it wouldn't be a trap."

Fussmouse Trap!!!

Tattymouse I told him. Times. But he didn't want to hear.

Fussmouse Traps, traps, traps! I don't want to hear about traps, either. I want reassurance.

Tattymouse He was always playing tricks with traps, was Charley.

Fussmouse Reassurance.

Tattymouse Taking the cheese without setting off the trap. Setting off the trap, then taking the cheese. He called it The Mousetrap Game.

Fussmouse Being able to sit down without first making sure the seat is there.

Tattymouse "You'll play that game once too often," I told him.

Fussmouse Being able to eat without wondering whether the food complies with all the regulations concerning hygiene and additives.

Tattymouse And he did.

Fussmouse Being able to sleep without wondering what may get at you once you've dropped off.

Tattymouse Bang it went and he screamed. Unless he screamed just before it went bang. Or the bang and the scream went together.

Fussmouse All my life I've been haunted by what may be lurking round the corner.

Tattymouse After that I never heard another thing. I don't know why. It may have been the noise. It may have been the shock. Or perhaps I'd heard all I'd ever want to hear.

Fussmouse If only somebody could assure me that everything's going to be all right.

Music

That's right.

Tattymouse Even if I could hear, I'd never hear *him* again, so what's the point?

Fussmouse (*struck by a sudden doubt*) Was that you, Tattymouse?

Tattymouse There's one big advantage to being deaf. You don't hear what you don't want to hear.

Fussmouse Tattymouse! (*Shaking her*) Was that you talking to me?

Tattymouse Mm? Sorry.

Fussmouse That's all right, then.

Tattymouse I was miles away.

Fussmouse I just thought it a reassuring thing for you to say. Quite unexpected and oddly comforting. I wish I could believe it. Do you believe it?

Tattymouse What did I say?

Music

Fussmouse You're so right.

Tattymouse Well, at any rate I promise not to mention Charley-mouse any more.

Fussmouse Say it again.

Music

If you say so . . .

Tattymouse After all, he's gone and we're here.

Fussmouse To sleep without wondering what I'll be waking up to.

Tattymouse At least we've got one another.

Music

Fussmouse (*yawning*) And so to bed.

Fussmouse drifts out

Tattymouse does not notice Fussmouse going

Tattymouse A mixed blessing sometimes, but you have to make the best of what you're left with. That's what I say.

Fussmouse (*off; distantly*) Hush, hush, wake up who dares. . . .

Tattymouse Not often, but I have been heard to say it. I shan't
miss any of you the way I miss Charleymouse and if that isn't a
blessing, what is it? I mean, whatever happens, not having to go
through so much missing again. At times like that one wishes
one *could* hear Grandmouse's Piper.

Music which Tattymouse does not hear

Once upon a time, my dears, there was this Piper. Oh, that's not
the unbelievable bit. Pipers were as common as breadcrumbs in
those days. What *was* unusual was this one combining music
with his job as pest control officer. Not that we mice ever were
pests, of course; but back in this particular once-upon-a-time
somebody decided there were just too many of us. So . . .

Music, louder now and more insistent. Tattymouse does not notice

What a pity that, as one gets old, one stops believing in fairy
stories. Besides, even in that story, one mouse has to be left to
tell the tale. Because if one hadn't been left, there'd have been
nobody left to pass the story on.

Music

I wonder how that one felt about it afterwards.

Music

I wonder if she sat waiting and waiting. Like this.

The music dies away into silence

What else was there to do?

CURTAIN

FURNITURE AND PROPERTY LIST

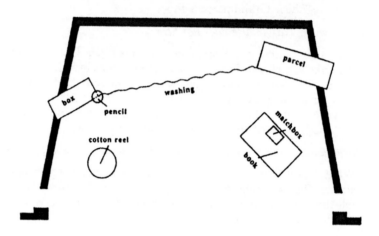

On stage: **Pencil**
Parcel
Matchbox } all "larger than life"
Book
Cotton reel

Washing (mouse size)

Other properties at the director's discretion

Printed by The Kingfisher Press, London NW10 7AS

Lightning Source UK Ltd.
Milton Keynes UK
UKOW05f0227170215

246377UK00001B/9/P